By Dingle Bay and
Blasket Sound

Steve MacDonogh

With Etchings and Drawings by Tomáisín Ó Cíobháin

BRANDON

First published 1991
Brandon Book Publishers Ltd,
Dingle, Co. Kerry, Ireland

Poems © Steve MacDonogh 1991

Etchings & drawings © Tomáisín Ó Cíobháin 1991

British Library Cataloguing in Publication Data
MacDonogh, Steve 1949 -
  By Dingle Bay and Blasket Sound
  1. English poetry
  I. Title
  821.914
  ISBN 0 86322 132 7

28/4/92

Typesetting and internal design: Brandon
Cover design: Steve MacDonogh and Jean McCord
Cover painting: 'San Inis by Tomáisín Ó Cíobháin
Printed by Colour Books Ltd, Dublin

for the emigrants from Corca Dhuibhne

ACKNOWLEDGEMENTS

The author wishes to acknowledge the editors of the following publications in which some of these poems first appeared:

Poetry Ireland Review, "New Irish Writing" (*Irish Press*), *Fortnight*, "New Irish Writing" (*Sunday Tribune*), *Salmon*, "Writing in the West" *(Connacht Tribune)*, *Irish Voice*, *Living Landscape Anthology* (West Cork Arts Centre), *Nantucket Review*, *Speak to the Hills* (Aberdeen University Press), *Stony Thursday Book*, *The Kerryman*.

Tomáisín Ó Cíobháin wishes to thank the Crawford College of Art and Design for their invaluable assistance.

CONTENTS

ILLUSTRATIONS

Lough Adoon and Ballyhoneen
below the Conor Pass:
there the land sings to him
songs of another self
to airs of a different world.
He puts on the clothes
he reserves for such occasions:
walking boots, thick socks,
twill trousers and anorak;
he places in a shoulder bag
nuts and fruit, dried and fresh.
He takes from the shelf
memories long unbidden,
dusts down names like
goirtín, páirc mhór,
fearann, páirc na croise.
He drives to Kilmore Cross,
and rough ground in Ballyhoneen
reveals at once stone walls
beneath the bog, field walls
of the first farming people.
Megaliths point his way
to neolithic graves and
bog myrtle yields its scent;
in wet ground green stars
fleshed with black spots,
petals of the Kerry violet
bearing the same name in Irish

as the liver-fluke.
Holly trees grow from a wedge grave
and a caher, but the island
is bare of all but the stone
of the Iron Age fort, or dún.
In Ballyhoneen in Corca Dhuibhne
all comes together – all,
that is, in the mind
where levels merge and he walks
horizons of a fuller self.
In Ballyhoneen in Corca Dhuibhne
below the Conor Pass
he casts off the everyday,
stands mid-stream below the waterfall
and contemplates a lake and a valley
the shape of his inner life.

COM AN ÁIR

At the Bar law rested uneasily
on foundations of colonial precedent.
Cabinets relied upon the permanence
of a declared State of Emergency.
But before this, a story of blood and silence.

There is a clinging taste in the mouth
of earth, of things about to be born.
Turf-brown rivers run slow across the plateau
before cascading at the lip of the ridge.
Pinguicula's violet flower wears
a green collar shaped like a star,
littered with dark jewels of prey.

The civil servant toyed idly with a signet ring
and outlined environmental implications
of the enforcement of EC guidelines.
On a building site a sharp Northern voice
carried from the office a passionate demand
for the observance of safety regulations.

Before this, a mountain track imitates
a river-bed bordered by turf banks
from which an ancient halberd protrudes
and multitudes of sharpened sticks of yew.
The shape of our history lies nascent:
if I penetrate the blanket bog
can I see the first farmers

begin to move up from the coasts,
along the rivers, above the tree-line
and into the peneplain resounding
to the generator hum of the wind
at Bearna na Gaoithe, the lofty
croak of raven, screech of falcon?

The cattle man shifted his cap back
with a thumb that paused at his lip,
adjusted his stance to the state of negotiations.

A history still unshaped, a story:
cattle like the black Kerry cow and,
equally small, the horses
move along the high valley
to the crossing points
of the mountains' spine.
It is a movement before nations,
before the name of Ireland.
There is no shade here,
nothing grows above knee height,
and even ten miles in the distance
the golden sweep of the bay
describes the bare shore
of a yet unpeopled sea.

Scaoilte Amach/Kerry Cows

My Love, My Country

We open to the world with morning light;
we wake to conflict, desire and discontent.
We have carried on a long time like this,
you and I, revisiting old quarrels,
ploughing new fields of disagreement.
Painfully unsure of each other, we are
suspicious, evasive and withdrawn.
We affect bland contentment, seek
to avoid the dark side of our world.
For lack of consensus we fear history;
wary of too much thought, we agree
with everything and nothing.
Every story is a series of sub-plots:
we don't know what directness is.
Every song is a form of lament:
we don't seek understanding.
To love truly we would have to trust
and trust is one thing we can never share.
And so we separate at times;
on meeting again enjoy brief closeness
before it all starts up again between us.
Evening falls towards night calmly, slowly:
it is orderly, assured, unquestioned, certain.
We open to the world with morning light
and wake to conflict, desire and discontent.

Trap Door

I am building Utopia in my loft.
Problem is, I can't get it down
to the rest of the house,
let alone out into the street
where others could share it.
The damn thing won't
fit through the trap door.

An braon atá thuas in uachtar leice go hárd, ag
titim im chluais agus fuaim na toinne le'm sháil.

Piaras Feirtéar

The mind's bias enters the heart,
spirals there; whatever way you move
it presses on you, snags, entwined.
A rock, a field, townland or cliff;
a road, a castle or island:
none is the elements of which it is forged.
The heart's forge fashions its own steel,
which strikes in its way at the nature of things,
strips like the sleán the skin
from the land, the intervening times,
and enters the past drawing blood.

A drop up there, on high, from the rocky roof,
falls into my ear and the waves sound at my heels.

Verses composed in a fugitive's cave;
notes of tradition that echo in stone cells.
Humanity walled by oppression
staggers to partial freedom
and builds new walls of fear.

In Cuas a'Bhodaigh Brendan's boat
still rises and falls with the swell.
We are all passengers on board,
forever failing to reach the open sea.

16

Ag Bórdáil/Preparing to Board

By Dingle Bay and Blasket Sound

In Ballyferriter in Corca Dhuibhne
the Three Sisters rear their heads to look
out over the endless expanse of the sea.
In Ballyferriter in Corca Dhuibhne
cohorts of German boy scouts
shade their eyes towards Atlantic sunset;
beside them a gaggle of girls from Dublin
pile into the bus for the Dún an Óir.
No one grows up in Ballyferriter
without having one eye on the horizon
where sky meets sea and clouds roll in.
No one looks at the outline of the "Dead Man";
no one watches the light change in the west
of an evening that moves from blue to yellow,
from yellow to gold, to pink, red and purple;
no one watches or looks without knowing
that on the far distant shore of the ocean
lies a new destination, a life and a home
in a place that will never be home.
In Daniel Keane's a Corkman plays fiddle,
a Yank talks folklore and a Dub sings;
at the bar three local men in their sixties,
their eyes sinking misty into pints.
There are Spaniards in the Blasket Sound,
seized by the great mouth of the sea
from ships of the Armada;
Blasket and mainland fishermen too,
pulled to death before their time.

And now it is the air that plucks
the young of Ballyferriter
not to death but to exile
from the gateways of farewell
at Shannon, Cork and Dublin.
No one grows up in Ballyferriter
without having one eye on the horizon,
or an ear to the phone for news from beyond
from sisters, brothers, friends...
And in the lands of opportunity
young emigrants dream
of becoming anything they wish,
yet know the reality of the possible.
But "home," they say, "is the only place
you can just be yourself."
Home is the deep and healing well
to which they return; and here
they pay the round and dance
like pilgrims at an old pattern.
Few see the reasons for their exile,
few want to know, it being enough
to learn a new place in a new world.
At home it is only brochures
and bureaucrats that brag
about the wonders of deep ploughs;
the rest register vegetables
rotting on the dump or ploughed back,
register an industry of excuses
for management expenses.
The confident promontory forts
express a proud, developed past,
but their ruins watch over

seas whose produce is stolen
and fields where buachalláin buí
is the only crop.
The people of Duibhne are scattering
while wide-boys and apparatchiks
bray like satisfied donkeys,
reaping funds in the name
of heritage and co-operation.
Language is turned on its head:
money gives power to liars,
makes fools of true women and men.
No one grows up in Ballyferriter
without having one eye on the horizon
where sky meets sea and clouds roll in.

Inis Tuaisceart/The Dead Man

Flowers from the living,
farewells to the dead:
as April shades into May
we're dragged back to winter
by the scairbhín.

scairbhín: from *garbhshíon*; rough weather. A
saying popular in Dingle is *Scairbhín na gCuach
is garbh í is is fuar.*

The hare with a saddle
presented itself to the man
footing turf at the top of the hill
and folded its back legs
to the seeping black ground.
The man, anonymous, dark,
a silhouette against the sky,
refused the offer of the saddle,
refused it again, and a third time.
In the mist of the mountain
the hare loomed ever larger
and the man broke and ran,
leaving his sleán behind him.
He ran over the rough ground
of the hill slope above his townland,
fled without looking back
until he reached his own house.
The hare followed him in:
he seized an iron from the fire
and thrust it glowing red
right between the hare's eyes.

One month later a woman
came begging at his door;
as she turned away he saw
light fall on her face to show
a bright red weal between her eyes.

That night as he walked the road
a silent funeral procession
approached from the hill;
he hid beneath the bridge
as a thousand mourners passed.
He followed to the graveyard
and saw the fresh-dug grave
and a headstone bearing his name.

St John the Baptist's Well, Kilmurry

There is a well, its approaches
strewn with cut bracken;
lightly dressed with stone
it stands sheltered by a tree.
The farmer parks his tractor,
leaves the engine running,
in the track between well and castle.

There is a well: he stands before it
after making nine rounds and throwing
nine blackberries picked from the hedges;
he stares into its waters.
John the Baptist hovers there,
a grey presence above his thoughts,
the waters a pool of absence
from the everyday, from labour.

One day of each year, one day
when blackberries are ripe he walks
a different land, bathes his heart
in waters no different
from springs on his own land
which are yet a door
to another dimension.
And then he returns over cut bracken
to the idling tractor.

"I'd rather wear an old mantle in Munster
than a torn silk gown in England."

Lord Essex

White bones earthed
under thin, green carpet
by kind, concealing centuries;
at this site of slaughter
wild wallflowers grow
where the roof once rested.
The heavy guns as they blasted
from Cathair na nAcraí
echoed between the headlands
of Kilmurry Bay, resounding
down the valley to startle
moorhen, snipe and heron.
Such massacre seems the bitter end,
the other side of that neat equation of
Elizabeth's Lord Essex.

There is a sketch of silence.

It is drawn from the moment,
from which the ripples now recede,
when a trout leapt
from the silvered stream
in sunless grey evening.
Its sound as it broke,
rose, flicked and fell
defined the silence
between rushes and flags
beneath blackthorn, bridge
and indeterminate sky.

CRÓ NA CAILLIGHE, BEARNA NA GAOITHE

On a cold bare hill stand
stone cabins of the two hags
where the wind throws its force
with the shape of the ridge:
the mountain does not yield
even to hold them in a hollow
but pins them to exposed wastes,
consigned by a myth born
in upland fields once fertile.
I walk beside their shadows
to find what lies in the legend
of death at the vast jaw of cliff,
wonder at names given to stones
when stories shortened winter nights.

A masonry stump
at the neck of Doon Point
stands above silurian rock
like a single standing stone,
a dark monolith before
the shrouded mass of Brandon.
Here, Pierce Ferriter
lamented Fitzgerald;
joined the resistance,
laying down his harp
to raise the sword
against the power of England.
Some of the music,
some of the poetry,
some of the politics
still sound in our ears,
carried on the turbulent
breeze or breath of centuries.
They are echoes passed and present,
relevant and redundant;
they are essences and leavings;
they are the words and notes
of a song in the hinterland
which swells as we stumble
into its ambit.
A masonry stump
at the neck of Doon Point
stands above silurian rock.

Geologists, holiday makers,
learners of Irish and archaeologists
pause and study in passing.
But as it stands against
the backdrop of Brandon
the very stones emit
cadences of what we are.

Clocháin, Fán/Clochans, Fahan

Like some gigantic coxcomb the arête
rises rock vast in ancient folds
and to its prow shape cling two walls
where long before imperial sword,
before bible and frock-coat,
long before canon and pike,
a giant hill-fort stood
proclaiming from its eagle height
that power lay with
the tribe that built it,
that unsurpassed, compelling power
resided with the gods
it was built to honour.
Here a stone head was buried
in ritual sacrifice for harvest;
here, too, funeral games were held
and history and law recited.
Ravens now hang immobile
close to the rock-sharp ridge,
high over the barren plain
and the river of the Fianna.
The walls of the fort have
slipped and fallen, sinking
imperceptibly into rock and turf
and over all is cast the constant
cloud of Brandon mountain.
From a distance the coxcomb rears,
the rest of head and neck obscured,

but even from miles away the fort stands out
when luck dresses rock with snow
and the knife-edge ridge gleams white
crossed by two black lines.
Benagh: these two strong walls
were stronghold of the tribe,
symbol of earthly power
and towering house of gods.

SHAG ROCK, KILMURRY BAY

Their angular heads
would be jade but for movement.
I close on a rock covered by fifty;
ship the oars – not too close
for fear of attack: white on flanks
signs of their mating season.
As the boat drifts closer
they start to leave their steep rest:
first awkward moment of take-off,
then elegant flight; now fifty question marks
bob in the mouth of Kilmurry Bay.

HOME GROUND

One cannot, he regretted,
speak well of a place always.
After all the PR men and publicists
have made their pence and left,
after smiles have been held for cameras,
achingly, and the last departing guest
has shaken hands for the last time,
he still remains curious, still
questions and passionately challenges.

One cannot, he regretted,
speak well of a place always.
Sing its praises by all means
as its particular music enfolds you;
find words for the unheard airs
that express the qualities of its people;
dance to the tunes spun out
in the everyday wonder of the place.
But in the end one cannot always
speak well of a place and be truthful.

"This seanchaí," said the teacher,
"unfortunately peppers his stories
with lewd and obscene material,
in place of which I have written
descriptions of the beautiful scenery."
After hearing a sermon on sex
a father of three daughters

mutters against the priest.
"Ah, now," says his neighbour,
"you can't be saying that."
"Don't you know yourself it's true?"
"True it may be, indeed, but
you wouldn't want to be saying it."

One cannot always praise:
favour is well regarded,
favour is even expected,
but praise and favour
unleavened by truth
is only the old plámás
and a species of condescension.

Walking from the pub after Mass,
a conversation in the rain:
"How's our heritage, Francis?"
"Wet, Jack, very bloody wet."
"We have good people in the town."
"We have some good ones all right!"

A man in his forties writes home:
"Why do you drive me each winter
to the hospital, electro-shock and drugs?"
He receives no reply but on visits
his relatives talk about funerals.

Returning daughters of the town
maintain vows of familial silence
about insights gained abroad;
butter wouldn't melt in their mouths

while they laugh behind their hands.
Their celebration is real enough,
love of the place is real enough
and so, too, is the hold of the world
beyond, the hold of working reality.
Home is safe haven, a sure resource
to be tapped and left unchanged.

One cannot speak well always
for true affection
hates complacency;
true affection stirs up and renews,
avoids the easy options,
the lines of least resistance.

Tourists batten on the place:
romantically inclined Germans speak
of the wondrous poverty of the people,
ignoring evidence of prosperity;
they listen to music played indifferently
and delight in having found
an experience *wirklich echt*.

Fishermen spin amicable yarns
over a drink or two, but when one
leaves the company antagonism
spills out and he's cut to shreds.
"No fisherman ever told the truth,"
says a cynic to general laughter,
"it's a tradition handed down.
And God help the poor woman
who loves a fisherman's son!"

One cannot always speak well:
praise yields approbation,
praise flatters and deceives,
praise leaves no room
for honest reflection,
glosses over with sentimentality
the true virtues of a place.
If one loves a place
he must hate it too,
hate its many transgressions.
Praise is a tactic
directed at weakness;
praise stultifies
and tells us nothing.

The place, like any other,
has its local tragedies, has
its frustrations and worse.
But in the end there are
few people more giving
and in few places exist
such ready acceptance,
such mundane ease;
if we sleep we sleep softly
and many may wish for less
without being safely dead.
Challenge is limited,
opportunities are restricted,
the economy requires
perpetual emigration;
yet those in London return and
feet that tread the streets of Boston
step lightly back on home ground.

At Caisleán Ghriaire the worm turned;
at Caisleán Ghriaire a serpent spoke.
That her husband killed her only fits
the stories that unfolded down the years.

I see her now: behind her as she stands
distance unseen in the eye of the dream –
an azure bay set in the sweep of the strand
flares like a skirt of blue and gold.

Her hands move in anger as she speaks,
fall to her side as she straightens, turns again.
I glimpse her across centuries, a firm face set
towards the sky, an image to touch the future.

LOCH NA MNÁ

They said that when young
she rose from the lake
and entered the mountain.

Whatever happened or
was believed to have happened,
she lived needing no man.

Neither one of the valley people
nor quite a creature of the mountain
she offered both threat and assurance.

Hope of abundance, fear of famine:
her presence at the end of the coum
seemed a guarantee of contradiction.

Often thought of as hand rested
on evening plough or spade, she was
a point about which life turned.

Her mystery she shared only
with the mountain she entered
when she rose from the lake.

Istigh sa Chom/Deep in the Coum

Night reared dark horse
warm southerly gale;
trees hedges moved urgently
against us the wind.
Distance hitting our drunkenness
would be luck house finding us
rather than ditch
moonlessness wrongfooting us
one step off the road;
which way back when hedges end
bog treelessness.
Unimpeded sound of force
wind breaking through nothing;
senseless battering drained;
even cottage light heartslifting
unbelievable before wind.
Finally in can only gasp at it.

Good grass of the hill slopes
is close-cropped now, bringing
profit at last from lambs
once a curse of poverty.
Above the fattening unit
in rough ground lies
Fionn's mother's grave:
I find only gorse and a wasps' nest
and am taken for a student –
who else would heed such a story?
But the farmer understands well enough
that cities teach strange ironies
and knows, too, that there's a living
even in poking white hands in rubble.
I catch a hint of condescension
towards one whose eyes
are turned backwards;
still less do his children respect
half-baked romantic illusions;
and while I ask about local songs
they turn to city sounds of punk.
Behind the new house's clean lines
stands the long dark and sunken shed
once the home built by the grandfather
who now mutters in his tea and spits,
the one dirty thing in the house.

Com Dubh Funeral

We buried the last of his name in that place.
I watched the lights of a hundred cars
mark the route of the old cart road
from the town below to the cross above;
later, the various proprieties observed,
headlight beams scattered from the valley;
and sitting alone in the old-style kitchen
I felt only muted sorrow, the sense of loss
yielding a soft cadence of selective memory.
Reaching for appropriate grief I found
ashes cold at last after fifty years or more.
In the clear morning bright snow
capped the grey spire of the ridge
where it rose from dark lake to the sky.
Perched on the slope at the butt of the hill,
small as a brown lichened boulder,
the cottage windows waited for winds,
its roof for rain and a few more years.
The house alone mocked nostalgia:
a monument to hardship, witness of betrayal,
from which a boy had left to fight the Tans,
had returned a man to observe, bewildered,
divisions of a new national order.
For it was a poor life he had lived always,
with little chance to change it,
and what was attempted remained
still uncompleted at the end.

Scamall sa Chom/Clouds Over the Coum

THE WRENBOYS

Hobby horse turns,
Captain strides,
sword in hand,
the fife, the fife:
sharp, piercing echoes;
the high notes tumble,
fall, rise again;
the sound rattles
against the insistent beat of drums.
Dark strawboys advance,
a car caught in the mêlée
must stand and deliver.
"Take her away down to the Quay,
we don't want her at all today."
Masked figures dance,
swirl in the darkness.
"All the boys they ran down Goat Street,
all the girls they made a plan."
Hobby's jaws snap
and children scream.
"All the boys they ran down Goat Street
to kill Sean Gould and the boody man."
Batman meets King Kong
under banners twisted by wind.
The ghosts of the Caseys
are marching with the Kerryman;
Paud Houlihan cries out,
"We never died a winter yet!"

The trip had me baffled at first:
your own place and your stride altered,
face forming expressions I'd not seen in the city.
Head jaunty, eyes quick yet relaxed,
you threw greetings in grand style,
sauntered at ease on your own streets.
But time had outweighed
home's intimacy, familiarity:
houses and people were not
as in your own time.
Absence and years had changed most things:
to those you'd known you spoke across a gap,
talked of a place no longer there
whose existence ever stood in doubt now.
Returning to the city, silence between us,
stories of escapades and characters told before
rang like mocking laughter in our heads.
When next I saw you again
you wore brash confidence like a suit,
sharp as a knife and just as cold;
it was the city or nothing now, and I
had seen you at too close a distance.

After rain from the west had laid
a moving blanket over the hours of morning
bees embedded themselves at noon
in every red hanging flower of fuchsia,
deserted for a while the bright stars of borage.
She wore her black hair long at that time,
hugged corners like some intimidated waif;
her pale face was a door closed against enquiry.
Bee orchids carpeted an unused meadow
and bugle nestled low in roadside ditches.
He heard third-hand half-tales about her,
soft sighs of neighbours carried messages of loss;
thinking her young to be another local tragedy,
he sighed himself and asked no further.
Winter gales uprooted an apple tree
overburdened with pale dead wood.
In the town social circles shrank with the cold
and the talk was all of funerals.
He did not see her pass in the street
nor encounter her in public house or shop.
Drying winds of March blew in:
the town stretched itself from sleep,
countryside wore new shades of green.
With her hair cropped in the Spring
she seemed a different person, or so he said
when he tried to understand why
he tracked persistently her erratic progress.
She seemed the spirit of the place then

and commanded streets she had haunted.
Yellow iris shouted from ditch and field,
gorse yielded honeyed almond scent.
Company crowded and events followed her:
she moved with ease, boldly unaware
of sudden power and beauty she possessed.
Purple loosestrife stood out against lush green,
sea pink formed soft mounds on rugged cliffs.
He paced the outskirts of her energy,
hung back from the electric storm
until sunlight again struck fire from fuchsia.

A Silver Coin

From the orange window we watch
day dawn on Cnoc an Chairn
and know that with the light
we may lie here no longer.

Last night your bare feet
on the stairs broke my sleep;
your out-of-doors cold skin
shocked me as ever wide awake.

You drew back the curtains
and the moon was a silver coin
which you placed around my neck,
attached by a silver chain.

The moon is a welcome friend
and holds our passion in its light,
but when sun hunts moon away
we may lie here no longer.

As you take your fugitive leave
we look out to the cloudless hill;
later we will swim at the beach,
meeting as if by accident.

Wars and famines are reported,
power games fashion headlines;
but until the world changes
we may lie here no longer.

Yesterday I sneezed
and down the sleeping town
it was reliably reported
I was dying of pneumonia.
Outside my house the walls
are blocked doorways of houses
deserted after the linen stopped.
Even forty years ago the street
burst daily with the colour
and din of children and their games;
its houses knocked from wall to wall
the music of flute and accordion.
But now there's some don't even
call the street by its own name
and the voices that once spun out rhymes
are mellowed and tell their tales
in Boston, Kilburn and New York.
Yet those who remain
still make a story of life,
still spin out yarns of who
said what to whom and when,
throw clusters of words
like iron filings to magnets,
group tales around a person;
on meeting exchange
not news but stories:
and truth, of course,
only carries a spear on stage.

A Fine Couple

He found that marriage possessed
the compelling attraction of combining
negative practicality with maudlin sentiment.

Knowing this and inhabiting the time and place
he slipped into haughty compliance,
preserving the alibi that he did it for her.

He wallowed in delusions of the past
while believing he was above all that
and walked down the aisle with a smirk.

But the laugh, of course, was on him:
as he slouched in atavistic arrogance
"the little woman" discovered herself.

He maintained the silence of perceived power
but was woken from surly reverie
to find she was a rebel in his camp.

At first best instincts asserted themselves,
then, finding no room for generosity,
he drew up lines of a fight he could not win.

Knowing hidden goodness he possessed
she reeled under the impact of his rage
but forced herself then to build her resistance.

She blamed herself for his behaviour:
feeling she had disturbed his equanimity
she said it was only right she should pay.

For a time they became a minor local scandal;
she developed her independence furtively,
he declined into morose drunkenness.

Guilt honed the blade of her strength;
she took command of their family
and the children wilted in face of her.

They may be seen now passing to Mass:
she to sing in the choir, he to stand in the porch;
in her wake he shuffles like a boy caught
        stealing.

Her absence, like summer's drought,
deceived and confused.
I mistook dry stream-beds
for turf tracks:
spring, when water had filled them,
lay beyond recall.

Her vision proved clearer and
in the height of summer
she pointed out where
streams ran underground,
showed me the lake which
still brimmed above.

Slow to understand, I stumbled
over rough ground until
she returned with winter;
and now from the stony hill
a hundred streams are flowing.

Ithir/The Field

Love slipped from me in a quiet hour:
a thousand tiny sounds built the hum of night;
the cat stretched and buried herself in sleep;
the painting of the mosque at Mastaba
stood on the mantelpiece between candles and
      roses.
In some unnoticed way emotions rearranged
      themselves;
the sinister twins of pain and longing vanished
      in the stillness,
leaving only the faint, dry perfume of regret;
a warm breeze billowed the folds of darkness.
In a quiet hour love slipped into the soft night.

A Music of Defeat

After a period of observation
a stockade was erected
piece by piece around me.
They smiled and talked as they worked
building the attractive enclosure.
Only later did I find
amongst potted plants at the perimeter
unyielding barbed wire emplacements.
She talked to me some days
across the barricades,
hung surreptitious ribbons
on the fence. But guards
were posted in the daytime then.
We retreated into night.
We strummed the fence-wire
in that benighted town
building a music of defeat
and woke with bloody fingers.

WIND

Wind: a drink with fishermen,
my bike can stay in the ditch.
Did you ever see a stream blown backwards?
A tower of foam at Ceann Sibéal:
a day like this brought the sea
that dragged her from rock haven.
Telegraph wires dance like strings of deranged
          puppets
at Feohanagh air screams past: I bend with it
and catch my breath fearing vacuum.
Did Cúchulainn cheat at Cathair Conraoí:
was his a wind-assisted leap?
The hills are hollow as the wind hits,
even the flatlands stretched like slender skin
make one long continuous bodhrán beat.
Between shoulders of hillside and hedge
the road crouches low at Mám na Gaoithe
then shouts with the blast from the harbour.
At home I hope the walls will hold:
will trees burst through the windows?
There's a herd of cattle on the roof.

Dorchú ar Bharra Liath/Dark Horizon

Night's City

She sat at the bare kitchen table
staring into a void beyond
white walls, declaring finally
that death must come quickly,
death to answer all assumptions.

Outside the broken glass
front door of her lodgings
she danced in another world,
ran through night's city,
weaving a blanket of sound,
of frantic dance and talk,
while the wheel of her mind
was spinning beyond control.

She stared across the table,
gazed through the wall behind him,
hand grasping firmly her cup
in the drowning clutch of despair.
Long hours of talk passed before
he forced her at last to hand up
the pain, surrender it to him.

Later she loved him briefly
for this forced surrender,
but she could never forgive him
for being there.
Now they sit at hostile distance,

unable even to exchange greetings.
If he faced her again across that table
he would still reach out
with the same movement to take
the cup from her hand; and she
would still curse him for ever.

MUINTIR NA GAELTACHTA

What's Peig to them now?
She might as well
have been from China.

The Irish language
is alive and well
and living in Boston.

You've got to be
a millionaire
to live on a Blasket island.

Ar an mBlascaod/On the Blasket

My lover is not here:
in her absence I drink whiskey
and wonder if she is drunk too.

I wear the clothes
she bought for me
and wonder when
she'll be here
to admire them.

Distance builds beautiful lies
to sweeten the breath of separation;
but there is fever in our thoughts:
distance burns us up.

Lithe and light
and strong like a dancer,
she nursed her pain
with selfless grace.
A card printed grey
and edged in black
told me of her death
too late for the funeral,
yet I needed in my own way
to celebrate her passing.
And so I took
a slow journey
through landscape shared,
a visiting of places in which...

With the miles I mark down
what I knew of her:
notches on a stick
like an ogham inscription
on the standing stone
of an ancient goddess
where I will celebrate
her funeral games.
The notches are marks
to register names of the dead
and I mark her down:
I, the living; she, the dead –
the boundary drawn

as national frontiers
could never be made
to separate us.

I embark now on
a wandering wake,
a wake of wandering.
Lahinch, Corofin,
Galway and Spiddal,
Ballisodare.
Once it was I
who deserted her
to other demands,
breaking a promise;
once it was she who
went suddenly missing:
Morocco
instead of Dingle.
One time clearly
each of us reneged
and yet no blame
hung between us.
At the Cliffs of Moher
the sea is her element,
the force that sustained her,
the force, too, that killed her.
At Corofin I learn
new facts of our separation;
learn, too, to dispel
the ghost that cries
"if only…"

At Ballisodare

the constant downpour
lifts for an hour.
In bright sunlight
such as she would have
captured on camera
I walk by the shore
where the corpses
of small green crabs
litter high water mark.
Our house nearby
has been repaired,
its garden immaculate
with small terraces
where once she and I
pulled up montbretia.
I walk across fields
and find the neighbour's house
boarded up and sightless
with hardboard windows.
The neighbour's dog
was called, absurdly,
Radio, and I catch now
a memory's glimpse
of Anne at the garden gate,
shaking with laughter,
as I stand at the corner
calling, "Radio, Radio!"

Lithe and light
and strong like a dancer,
I celebrate her here
at the edge of the bay
of Ballisodare.

MID-PASSAGE TRAUMA

for Pat

The breach is down, so I go now;
whatever wish I leave behind...
Pain repeats, a fist like a stone
in a delicate part of the brain,
and now I'm wandering, wondering,
by now I need to know
will no one, no two be guides;
the senses
cannot speak, cannot write:
will I hate what I loved before?
Oh, sing me a song, give me a line:
let the sound of it penetrate;
tell me a story please
but play your tune well
or I go down empty
to the river, to the grand canal,
to the estuary, to nowhere, to where
the road was swept by some tide
that never rose before;
telegraph lines are down,
senses blown to the wind;
I fight against violence,
chaos and rage, fight
to reach the avenue of grief
and find a tree felled by a storm,
already stripped of leaves.

RITE OF PASSAGE

for N.D.

I woke from dreams of loss,
pathetically spitting
like stale bread from a dry mouth
curses at your intrusion.
I thought myself abandoned,
streets stood indifferent.
I imagined the parting of a sea
but instead of miraculous passage
I saw blocked water well up,
a poisonous dark flood.
I removed all paintings and posters,
made a bed on the floor with a single sheet.
I explored avenues where gaunt trees
were skeletons of sentiment.
In a bus I hid in the back seat
from children, wives and husbands.
The tragedies told by headlines
were unheard echoes in the distance.
On O'Connell Bridge blue-helmetted cops
moved in on seated figures in the rain:
a boy screamed and went sprawling:
I stepped over him to sit beside you.

There is a temptation
in a town where gossip
is the first language
to go anywhere about our business,
tailoring behaviour
to social expectations;
a temptation to package emotions,
to fly from honesty in love,
striking passionless bargains
to subdue the senses.
There is plenty to distract us:
music, drink and company,
an endless social round
of mutual complicity;
and in our lives we conspire
in continuous surrender
of the human title.

I am the prospective lover:
not knowing you yet
I pause before my door,
appalled at what may be revealed.

Butterfly City

for Shay, who asked why

In Butterfly City tribes gathered
demanding every day and night
new entertainments, fresh diversions.
In Butterfly City musicians played
till they could play no more,
dancers danced till they fell
to the ground or into each others' arms.
In front and back rooms of bars
spirits soared and blood raced
to sounds of fiddle and guitar;
talk came in instrumental riffs
while children raised seductive faces
repeating demands that were and were not met,
declining then in late night tiredness
to lean pale-faced on adult knees
like so many casualties of war.
Passions glowed and flamed then
and grew bold on drink
which also later tamed them,
leaving room in the morning
for the distance of shrugged farewells.
Butterfly City, high on talk and craic
Butterfly City, high on dope and drink,
on sex and on yourself; sure everyone
wants to know you when you're high.
The longer you can stretch the nights

the longer you can put off mornings
when no one wants to hear your blues,
stave off the hour in which
you look death in the face
and think you see a friend.
Butterfly City, your songs of joy
are frantic from fear of sadness.
Butterfly City, you lift me up
and I fly with you, but oh the fall
when your beautiful, fragile wings collapse!

HALF-STRANGER FRIEND

for E.

Where water flowed full flood
he found her, face etched
with despair as winter sun
struck lines from buildings
and failed to blunt the edge
of a north-east wind that rivalled
the force of the Corrib river.
Talk loosened the knot of tension,
eased out the pain of unseen wires
binding sinews of feeling
in the cramp of self-destruction.
He might have told her to block her ears
to siren calls of hollow laughter
and insistence that she share the craic,
might have said there must be more
to life than seven drunken nights a week;
but instead he asked that she value herself
only as much as he did, a half-stranger friend.
When they parted she walked swinging her arms
along the street beside the thundering Corrib.
And a man leaned on his bar counter,
as laden with listening, as leaden with sorrow
as the clouds that blew in to smother the sun.

You were not surprised
at the lines of the unemployed,
at their sullen violence and
the daylight street confrontations.
You were not surprised
to find the city gone in the teeth,
open-mouthed with shock,
its veins all burst.
You were not surprised
at the sound of curfew sirens,
the howl of the night
in cavernous commercial streets.
You were not surprised
at sudden night raids,
at tanks, soldiers, guns,
armoured cars and snatch squads.
You were not surprised
even when snipers opened up
and mortars thumped
from the hills above.
So why were you so surprised
when you arrived at their house
and found them making love?

1.

Cast the first stone quickly
for fear of becoming a target.
Keep the prospect of suffering at bay:
despise those who suffer in public.
You may expect no compassion,
so extend none to others.
Judge loudly to discourage
others from judging you.
Believe always the worst of everyone
the better to parade your virtue.
Don't stick your neck out:
you might lose your head.
Tell jokes about others' misfortunes:
let laughter drown your fears.

2.

Leaving fields, houses and work
they came on frozen roads:
neighbours who saw one of their own
tormented by an alien law.

They rallied behind no heroine,
stood in support of no angel,
but cast their lot with a person
as fallible as the rest of us.
Humanity asserted itself
not in loud blazons of principle
but in simple solidarity.
Yellow roses were the show,
firm handshakes the substance.

Also from Brandon

Steve MacDonogh
A Visitor's Guide to the Dingle Peninsula

"Marvellous... a comprehensive and extremely readable blend of Dingle history and tourist guide. It not only tells the reader where, when and how to see the sights but also includes an accompanying history of that fascinating area, replete with detailed maps." *Boston Irish Echo*

"It is a splendid production, lavishly illustrated with photographs and clearly drawn maps, and it has been written with gusto, information and lore pouring from every page." *Cork Examiner*

"This is a great item for the tourist, antiquarian, language student, thirsty drinker or holy pilgrim. It is not like other, short-weight guidebooks. It lets history hang out all over where you can get at it." *Irish Edition*, Philadelphia

Steve MacDonogh
Green and Gold: The Wrenboys of Dingle

"Interesting and excellently produced... compulsive reading... an excellent, entertaining book." *Books Ireland*

"The first complete documentation of the event... it is important in that it charts in some detail one of our great traditions and so, in time, it will itself become part of our folklore. It is written lightly, with that touch of wry Kerry humour which appeals, and is well illustrated." *Cork Examiner*

SEAN MANNION
IRELAND'S FRIENDLY DOLPHIN

"Fungie, the wild but friendly dolphin, popped up in Dingle Harbour, stayed for seven years and delighted everyone lucky enough to come in contact with him. Sean Mannion observed the charming escapades of Fungie over a three-year period and we can now share the fun in his lavishly illustrated book." *Evening Herald*

"The lore of sea mammals, the biology of the dolphin and the life of West Kerry are some of the topics covered in this most attractive and deeply researched book." *RTE Guide*

DAVID GREENE & FRANK O'CONNOR
A GOLDEN TREASURY OF IRISH POETRY,
AD 600-1200

"This excellent volume... a combined operation by a scholar and a translator of the first rank. Greene's introduction is a model guide to the subject and his comments on the chosen poems are distinguished for their uncluttered thinking." *Irish Press*

"This outstanding collection of poems, translations, individual commentaries and a general introduction." *Ireland of the Welcomes*

"One of the most memorable Irish books.... The cull from 600 to 1200 is strikingly rich and sophisticated." *Irish Independent*